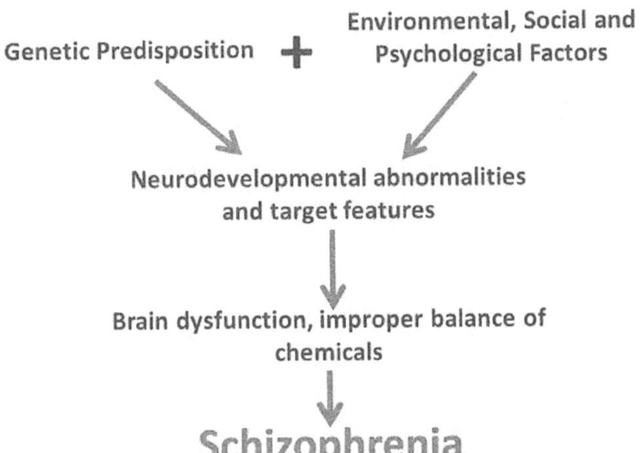

Genetic Predisposition
+
Environmental, Social and Psychological Factors
Neurodevelopmental abnormalities and target features
Brain dysfunction, improper balance of chemicals
Schizophrenia

I0695934

Inside Schizophrenia:

Exploring the Mind, Symptoms and Treatments

Migdalia Mugan

Table of content

Introduction: Navigating the Mosaic of Schizophrenia

In the vast tapestry of human experiences, few conditions are as intricate, multifaceted, and enigmatic as schizophrenia. This book invites you to embark on a journey—a journey that traverses the complexities of this disorder, unravels its mysteries, and illuminates the lives of those who navigate its challenges with courage and resilience.

Schizophrenia, often misunderstood and misrepresented, is far more than a clinical diagnosis. It's a condition that affects individuals, families, and communities, touching every aspect of a person's life. From the intricate interactions of genetics and environment to the transformative power of treatment and support, this book aims to shed light on every facet of schizophrenia, offering insights, stories, and perspectives that broaden our understanding.

Each chapter delves into a different facet of the disorder, guiding you through its origins, symptoms, diagnostic journey, treatment strategies, and the power of human connection. We'll explore the intricacies of genetics and environmental factors that contribute to its emergence. We'll step into the shoes of those who live with schizophrenia, sharing their personal stories of triumph, struggle, and hope. We'll challenge the stigma that often surrounds mental health conditions, and we'll celebrate the advancements in research and treatment that offer pathways to healing.

Throughout this exploration, you'll encounter the voices of individuals who have walked the path of schizophrenia—individuals who have faced stigma, defied odds, and carved out meaningful lives despite the challenges. You'll meet caregivers, friends, and advocates who contribute to the support networks that sustain those affected by the disorder.

Schizophrenia, like any other facet of the human experience, is a mosaic of stories, insights, and emotions. This book aspires to provide a comprehensive view of this intricate mosaic, fostering empathy, understanding, and the drive for change. By the time you turn the final page, it is our hope that you will not only have gained knowledge but also a deeper appreciation for the resilience and strength of those who journey through the complexities of schizophrenia.

Together, we embark on a journey of learning, compassion, and advocacy—a journey that leads us to a place of greater understanding and connection. Let us navigate this tapestry of schizophrenia with open hearts and open minds, guided by the conviction that every story deserves to be heard, every voice deserves to be respected, and every life touched by schizophrenia deserves the opportunity to thrive.

Chapter 1: Unveiling Schizophrenia: Exploring the Enigmatic Mind

In the labyrinth of human consciousness, where thoughts weave intricate patterns and emotions flow like currents, lies the enigmatic realm of schizophrenia. This chapter sets the stage for our journey through the intricate tapestry of this mental disorder, delving into its definition, historical context, and the profound impact it has on individuals and society.

Defining Schizophrenia: Beyond Labels

Schizophrenia, a term derived from the Greek words "schizo" (split) and "phrene" (mind), conjures images of a fractured reality. Yet, its meaning goes beyond a mere partitioning of the mind. Schizophrenia is a chronic mental disorder that disrupts an individual's thoughts, emotions, perceptions, and behaviors. It's a condition where the boundaries between reality and imagination blur, where the symphony of the mind plays discordant notes.

A Historical Odyssey: From Ancient Beliefs to Modern Understanding

The history of schizophrenia is as complex and varied as the disorder itself. Throughout the ages, different cultures and societies interpreted its symptoms in diverse ways. Ancient civilizations attributed the voices and visions to the influence of gods, while medieval times saw them as possessions by evil spirits. It wasn't until the late 19th century that Emil Kraepelin and Eugen Bleuler laid the foundations for our modern understanding, coining the term "schizophrenia" and recognizing its clinical patterns.

A Global Presence: The Prevalence of Schizophrenia

Schizophrenia is not confined to a specific region, culture, or socioeconomic background. It spans the globe, affecting millions of individuals and their families. While its prevalence varies across different populations, it is estimated that about 1% of the world's population experiences schizophrenia at some point in their lives. This prevalence highlights the significance of our endeavor to understand and address this complex disorder.

The Impact: A Ripple Effect on Individuals and Society

Beyond its clinical manifestations, schizophrenia leaves an indelible mark on individuals, families, and communities. Relationships strained by the disorder's challenges, educational and occupational aspirations disrupted, and dreams altered—schizophrenia reverberates far beyond the individual diagnosed. Society itself grapples with the repercussions, from the burden on healthcare systems to the pervasive stigma that can isolate those affected.

As we embark on this exploration of schizophrenia, it's essential to recognize that behind every diagnosis lies a unique story—a story of courage, resilience, and hope.

The chapters that follow will delve into the depths of symptoms, causes, treatments, and the journeys of those touched by schizophrenia. Through understanding and empathy, we aim to illuminate the path toward improved support, reduced stigma, and a brighter future for all individuals navigating the enigmatic landscape of schizophrenia.

Schizophrenia is a complex and chronic mental health disorder that affects a person's thoughts, emotions, perceptions, and behavior. It often impairs an individual's ability to think clearly, manage emotions, and interact with others in a meaningful way. Schizophrenia is characterized by a range of symptoms that can vary in severity and duration.

Key symptoms of schizophrenia can be categorized into three main groups:

Positive Symptoms: These are experiences that are present in individuals with schizophrenia but not usually experienced by others. They include:

- Hallucinations: Perceiving things that are not present, such as hearing voices or seeing things that others do not.
- Delusions: Holding false beliefs that are resistant to reason or

- *Contradictory evidence*: Delusions can involve paranoia, grandiosity, or beliefs of being controlled by external forces.

- **Disorganized Thinking**: Individuals with schizophrenia may have difficulty organizing their thoughts, leading to speech that is fragmented or incoherent.

- **Disorganized or Abnormal Motor Behavior**: This may manifest as unpredictable behavior, bizarre movements, or a lack of responsiveness.

Negative Symptoms: These refer to a reduction or absence of normal functioning that is usually present in individuals without schizophrenia.

Negative symptoms include:

- **Flat Affect**: A reduced range of emotional expression, often leading to a lack of emotional responsiveness

- **Reduced Speech**: Individuals may speak very little, providing only brief or monosyllabic answers.

- **Anhedonia**: The inability to experience pleasure or interest in previously enjoyable activities.

- **Alogia**: A decrease in the amount of speech or the quality of speech, often characterized by poverty of speech.

Cognitive Symptoms: These are disruptions in cognitive functions that affect memory, attention, and problem-solving abilities. Cognitive symptoms can have a significant impact on daily functioning and quality of life.

The onset of schizophrenia usually occurs in late adolescence or early adulthood, and the exact cause is not fully understood.

Genetic factors, brain structure abnormalities, neurotransmitter imbalances (particularly involving dopamine), and environmental factors may all contribute to the development of the diagnosis that is typically made based on the presence of specific symptoms over a certain period of time.

Treatment for schizophrenia often involves a combination of antipsychotic medications, psychotherapy, psychosocial interventions, and support from a multidisciplinary team.

It's important to note that while schizophrenia is a chronic disorder, many individuals can experience significant improvements in symptoms and lead fulfilling lives with proper treatment and support.

Early intervention, adherence to treatment plans, and a supportive network of family and friends are crucial factors in managing the condition.

The Diagnosis Process of Schizophrenia: Unraveling Complexities

Diagnosing schizophrenia is a complex and nuanced process that requires careful assessment, collaboration among healthcare professionals, and consideration of various factors. Since the disorder presents with a wide range of symptoms and can mimic other conditions, the diagnosis process involves thorough evaluation, ruling out alternative explanations, and understanding the individual's unique experiences.

Clinical Evaluation:

Initial Assessment:

The diagnosis journey typically begins with an individual seeking help due to distressing symptoms. A mental health professional, such as a psychiatrist or clinical psychologist, conducts an initial assessment to gather information about the individual's experiences, symptoms, and medical history.

Symptom Profiling:
Schizophrenia is characterized by a combination of positive, negative, and cognitive symptoms.
Positive symptoms include hallucinations, delusions, and disorganized thinking.
Negative symptoms involve diminished emotional expression, social withdrawal, and lack of motivation.
Cognitive symptoms encompass difficulties in concentration, memory, and decision-making.

Rule Out Other Conditions:

Differential Diagnosis:

The diagnostic process includes ruling out other medical or psychiatric conditions that can present with similar symptoms. Conditions like bipolar disorder, schizoaffective disorder, substance-induced psychosis, and certain medical conditions need to be considered and differentiated from schizophrenia.

Medical Examination:

A thorough medical evaluation is essential to identify any medical conditions or substances that may contribute to the symptoms. Medical conditions such as brain tumors, epilepsy, and autoimmune disorders can sometimes manifest with psychotic features.

Duration and Impairment:

Duration of Symptoms:

Schizophrenia diagnosis requires that symptoms persist for a significant portion of time. These symptoms often continue for at least six months, including a period of active-phase symptoms. This duration helps distinguish the disorder from brief psychotic episodes.

Functional Impairment:

The symptoms of schizophrenia must cause significant impairment in various areas of the individual's life, including work, school, relationships, and self-care.

Collateral Information:

Family and Social History:

Gathering information from family members, close friends, or caregivers can provide insight into the individual's history and the progression of symptoms. It helps form a comprehensive picture of the person's experiences.

Developmental History:

Understanding the individual's developmental milestones, childhood experiences, and any traumatic events can contribute to a more accurate diagnosis.

Diagnostic Criteria:

DSM-5: The fifth edition of the Diagnostic and Statistical Manual of Mental Disorders (DSM-5) provides standardized criteria for diagnosing schizophrenia. The DSM-5 outlines specific diagnostic criteria based on the presence and duration of symptoms. Subtypes and Specifiers: The DSM-5 categorizes schizophrenia into different subtypes and specifiers based on symptom presentation, such as paranoid, disorganized, catatonic, undifferentiated, and residual subtypes.

Multidisciplinary Approach:

Collaborative Assessment:
 Diagnosing schizophrenia often involves a multidisciplinary team of mental health professionals, including psychiatrists, psychologists, social workers, and psychiatric nurses. This collaboration ensures a comprehensive and accurate assessment.

Cultural Considerations:

Cultural Sensitivity: Cultural factors can influence the expression and interpretation of symptoms. Mental health professionals need to consider cultural norms, beliefs, and language barriers during the diagnosis process.

Long-Term Monitoring:

Longitudinal Assessment: The diagnosis process is not a one-time event. Ongoing monitoring and assessment are necessary to track the individual's symptoms, response to treatment, and overall well-being.

Conclusion:

Diagnosing schizophrenia involves a meticulous and patient-centered approach.

Healthcare professionals must consider a range of factors, collaborate with multidisciplinary teams, and carefully assess symptoms and impairment.

While the process may be complex, an accurate diagnosis is essential for developing effective treatment plans and supporting individuals in their journey towards better mental health and quality of life.

Schizophrenia Statistics: A Comprehensive Overview

Schizophrenia is a complex mental health disorder that impacts millions of individuals worldwide. Understanding the prevalence, demographic patterns, and global impact of schizophrenia is essential for effective healthcare planning, treatment, and support systems. Here are some key statistics that shed light on the scope of the disorder:

Global Prevalence:

Prevalence: Schizophrenia affects approximately 20 million people worldwide. The prevalence varies by region and may be influenced by factors such as genetics, socioeconomic conditions, and access to healthcare.

Incidence: The incidence of schizophrenia is estimated to be around 15 per 100,000 people each year. It usually emerges during late

adolescence or early adulthood, although
onset can occur at any age.

Demographics:

Gender: Schizophrenia occurs equally in both
genders, but there are some gender-related
differences in symptom presentation. Men
tend to experience symptoms at a slightly
younger age than women.

Age of Onset: While the disorder can
manifest at any age, most cases of
schizophrenia develop between late
adolescence and the early 30s. Onset after the
age of 45 is less common.

Global Burden:

Disability-Adjusted Life Years (DALYs):
Schizophrenia ranks among the top 20 causes
of disability worldwide. DALYs are a measure
that combines years of life lost due to

premature death and years lived with disability.

Economic Impact: Schizophrenia places a substantial economic burden on individuals, families, and society. The costs include medical expenses, lost productivity, and indirect costs due to caregiving and social support.

Geographic Patterns:

Regional Differences: The prevalence and impact of schizophrenia vary across regions. Developing countries may have higher rates of treatment gaps, limited access to mental health resources, and stigma-related challenges.

Urbanization: Some studies suggest that urban environments may be associated with an increased risk of developing schizophrenia. Factors such as social isolation, stress, and exposure to pollutants could contribute to this association.

Comorbidity:

Substance Use: Co-occurring substance use disorders are common among individuals with schizophrenia. Substance abuse can exacerbate symptoms, complicate treatment, and contribute to poorer outcomes.

Physical Health: Individuals with schizophrenia have an increased risk of developing physical health conditions such as obesity, diabetes, cardiovascular diseases, and respiratory disorders.

Treatment Gap:

Access to Treatment: A significant treatment gap exists, particularly in low- and middle-income countries, where access to mental health services is limited. Many individuals with schizophrenia do not receive appropriate diagnosis or treatment.

Adherence Challenges: Adherence to medication regimens can be challenging for individuals with schizophrenia. Factors such as side effects, lack of insight into the illness, and stigma may contribute to non-adherence.

Stigma and Discrimination:

Social Stigma: Stigma surrounding schizophrenia can lead to social isolation, discrimination, and barriers to employment and education. Stigmatization can exacerbate the challenges faced by individuals with the disorder.

Family Impact: Schizophrenia also affects families and caregivers, who may experience emotional distress, financial strain, and disruptions in their own lives.

Advances in Research and Treatment:

Research Progress: Advances in neuroscience, genetics, and technology have led to a deeper understanding of the neurobiological underpinnings of schizophrenia. This knowledge informs the development of more targeted treatments.

Treatment Innovation: Treatment approaches for schizophrenia continue to evolve, with a focus on personalized medicine, cognitive remediation, psychotherapy, and early intervention strategies.

Conclusion:

The statistics surrounding schizophrenia reflect the
global impact of the disorder on individuals, families,
and societies.
Improved awareness, early intervention, increased
access to mental health services, and reduced stigma
are crucial steps toward enhancing the quality of life
for those affected by schizophrenia.

Chapter 2: Symptoms and Subtypes: Navigating the Landscape of Schizophrenia

Within the intricate tapestry of schizophrenia lies a diverse array of symptoms, each contributing to a complex and unique experience for those affected. This chapter delves into the multifaceted nature of schizophrenia symptoms, exploring their categories, manifestations, and the role they play in shaping the lives of individuals living with the disorder.

Positive Symptoms: A Kaleidoscope of Unconventional Experiences

Schizophrenia often manifests through a spectrum of positive symptoms that introduce an element of distortion to an individual's perception of reality. Hallucinations, whether auditory, visual, or tactile, can cause one to hear voices, see unreal images, or feel sensations that others cannot. Delusions, false beliefs that persist despite evidence to the contrary, contribute to a perception of the world that may seem surreal or baffling.

Negative Symptoms: The Void Within

In contrast to positive symptoms, negative symptoms involve the absence or reduction of normal functions. These symptoms often impact a person's ability to engage with the world around them. Social withdrawal, diminished emotional expression, and anhedonia—the inability to experience pleasure—contribute to a sense of detachment and isolation. Motivation wanes, leading to decreased interest in previously enjoyed activities.

Cognitive Symptoms: Struggles Within Thought's Maze

Cognitive symptoms, perhaps less visible but equally significant, affect thinking processes. Impaired attention, memory, and executive functions can make even routine tasks challenging. Individuals may struggle to concentrate, plan, and organize their thoughts. This cognitive fog, coupled with other symptoms, can hinder the ability to communicate effectively and navigate daily life.

Exploring Schizophrenia Subtypes: A Tapestry of Diversity

Within the spectrum of schizophrenia lies an array of subtypes, each presenting a distinctive pattern of symptoms. Paranoid schizophrenia is marked by delusions of persecution, while disorganized schizophrenia manifests through incoherent speech and behavior. Catatonic schizophrenia involves motor disturbances, while undifferentiated and residual subtypes exhibit a combination of various symptoms.

Paranoid Schizophrenia: Unraveling the Intricacies of Suspicion and Hallucinations

Schizophrenia, a multifaceted mental health disorder, manifests in various forms, each with its own distinct characteristics. One of these forms is paranoid schizophrenia, a subtype that revolves around intense feelings of suspicion, delusions, and hallucinations. It presents a unique set of challenges for individuals affected by the disorder and those who care for them.

Understanding Paranoid Schizophrenia

Paranoid schizophrenia is characterized by prominent symptoms of paranoia, which involves extreme and unwarranted suspicion of others, often accompanied by auditory hallucinations and delusional thinking. Individuals with this subtype may believe that others are plotting against them, spying on them, or intending harm. These delusions can be persistent and deeply ingrained, leading to a profound impact on their thoughts, behaviors, and emotions.

Hallucinations and Delusions

Hallucinations are a hallmark of paranoid schizophrenia, particularly auditory hallucinations where individuals hear voices that are not real. These voices can be critical, commanding, or conversational. Delusions experienced by individuals with paranoid schizophrenia often center around themes of persecution, reference, or grandiosity. They may feel targeted, believe that events or actions hold personal significance, or hold inflated beliefs about their own abilities.

Impact on Daily Life

The symptoms of paranoid schizophrenia can significantly affect an individual's daily life. The constant suspicion and distress caused by delusions can lead to social withdrawal, difficulty forming relationships, and a reduced ability to function in work or educational settings. The hallucinatory experiences may also contribute to anxiety, depression, and isolation.

Diagnosis and Differential Diagnosis

Diagnosing paranoid schizophrenia involves observing the presence of characteristic symptoms over a significant period. It's essential to differentiate it from other conditions that might share similar symptoms, such as other types of schizophrenia, mood disorders, or even substance abuse.

Treatment Approaches

The treatment of paranoid schizophrenia typically involves a combination of antipsychotic medications, psychotherapy, and psychosocial interventions. Medications aim to manage the symptoms of paranoia, delusions, and hallucinations. Psychotherapy, such as Cognitive-Behavioral Therapy

(CBT), can help individuals challenge their delusional beliefs and learn coping strategies. Psychosocial interventions focus on improving daily life skills, social interactions, and overall well-being.

Challenges in Treatment

Treatment of paranoid schizophrenia can be challenging due to the intense nature of the delusions and the suspicion that accompanies them. Individuals with this subtype may be reluctant to accept treatment, believing that interventions are part of a conspiracy against them. Building trust, providing a supportive environment, and involving family members in treatment planning are crucial steps.

A Holistic Approach

Holistic approaches, encompassing physical health, nutrition, exercise, and stress management, can complement traditional treatment strategies. A healthy lifestyle can contribute to better overall well-being and support symptom management.

Living with Hope

While living with paranoid schizophrenia can be challenging, many individuals can find relief from their symptoms with appropriate treatment and support. The journey towards managing the disorder involves embracing a comprehensive treatment plan, building a supportive network, and fostering an understanding environment.

In the realm of paranoid schizophrenia, understanding the intricate interplay of delusions, hallucinations, and suspicion is key. By shedding light on this subtype, we can foster empathy, challenge misconceptions, and contribute to a more informed and compassionate approach to supporting individuals living with paranoid schizophrenia.

Disorganized Schizophrenia: Unraveling the Complexity of Thought and Behavior

Schizophrenia, a complex mental health disorder, encompasses several subtypes, each characterized by distinct patterns of symptoms. Among these subtypes is disorganized schizophrenia, which is marked by profound disruptions in thought processes, emotions, and behaviors. Understanding the intricacies of disorganized schizophrenia is essential for comprehending its impact on individuals and guiding effective interventions.

The Essence of Disorganized Schizophrenia

Disorganized schizophrenia, also known as hebephrenic schizophrenia, is characterized by disorganization of thought, speech, and behavior. Individuals with this subtype often exhibit a lack of coherent thought patterns, making it challenging for them to communicate effectively. Disorganized behavior, emotional blunting, and flat affect are also prominent features of this subtype.

Cognitive Disarray

A hallmark of disorganized schizophrenia is the presence of disorganized thinking. Thoughts may jump from one unrelated topic to another, creating incoherent speech patterns known as "word salad." Tangentiality, where conversations stray from the original topic, and loose associations, where connections between thoughts are weak, are common. This cognitive disarray makes it difficult for individuals to communicate their ideas coherently.

Emotional Fluctuations

Individuals with disorganized schizophrenia may experience rapid and unpredictable shifts in emotions. Their affect can be flat, with minimal emotional expression, or inappropriate, where their emotional response does not match the situation. This emotional instability can further hinder effective communication and interpersonal interactions.

Bizarre Behavior

Disorganized behavior is a key aspect of this subtype. Individuals may engage in peculiar or purposeless actions, showing little regard for social norms. Daily tasks such as personal hygiene and organization may be neglected, contributing to impaired functioning. Disorganized behavior can be socially isolating and increase the individual's vulnerability.

Impairment in Daily Functioning

Disorganized schizophrenia often results in significant impairment in daily life. Individuals may struggle to hold a job, maintain relationships, or even manage basic self-care tasks. This can lead to a dependency on caregivers and contribute to feelings of frustration and low self-esteem.

Diagnosis and Differential Diagnosis

Diagnosing disorganized schizophrenia involves evaluating the presence of disorganized thinking, speech, and behavior over a significant period. Differential diagnosis is crucial to distinguish disorganized schizophrenia from other conditions with similar symptoms, such as other schizophrenia subtypes or mood disorders.

Treatment and Challenges

Treatment for disorganized schizophrenia involves a combination of antipsychotic medications, psychotherapy, and psychosocial interventions. Medications aim to manage symptoms, while therapy focuses on improving communication skills, social interactions, and daily functioning. Challenges may arise due to difficulties in engaging with treatment and addressing the disorganized thinking patterns.

Supportive Environment

Creating a supportive environment is vital for individuals with disorganized schizophrenia. Family members, caregivers, and mental health professionals play a pivotal role in providing consistent support, encouraging treatment adherence, and fostering understanding.

Fostering Empathy and Compassion

Understanding the intricacies of disorganized schizophrenia is a step towards fostering empathy and compassion for those living with this subtype. By acknowledging the challenges posed by disorganized thinking and behavior, we can contribute to reducing stigma and creating a more inclusive society.

In delving into the depths of disorganized schizophrenia, we gain insight into the complexity of thought, emotion, and behavior that individuals experience. By shedding light on this subtype, we pave the way for increased awareness, empathy, and effective interventions that empower individuals with disorganized schizophrenia to lead fulfilling lives.

Catatonic Schizophrenia: Unraveling the Enigma of Motor Disturbances

Within the spectrum of schizophrenia, catatonic schizophrenia stands as a distinctive subtype defined by its pronounced motor disturbances and unique symptom profile. This subtype is characterized by extremes in movement, ranging from immobility to excessive, purposeless activity. Understanding the complexities of catatonic schizophrenia is essential for grasping its impact on individuals and guiding effective approaches to care.

The Essence of Catatonic Schizophrenia

Catatonic schizophrenia is marked by disruptions in motor behavior, speech, and emotional expression. Individuals with this subtype can alternate between states of immobility, known as catatonic stupor, and agitated, hyperactive behavior. These extreme motor manifestations can greatly impede an individual's ability to interact with their environment and engage in daily activities.

Motor Disturbances

A defining feature of catatonic schizophrenia is the presence of motor disturbances that range from severe underactivity to excessive and uncontrolled movements. Catatonic stupor is characterized by a state of almost complete immobility, where individuals may remain motionless for extended periods. Conversely, catatonic excitement involves hyperactivity, purposeless movements, and even potentially harmful behaviors.

Negativism and Waxy Flexibility

Individuals with catatonic schizophrenia may exhibit negativism, where they resist any attempts to be moved or manipulated. This can manifest as resistance to simple actions, such as changing positions or performing routine tasks. Waxy flexibility is another phenomenon where individuals can be molded into specific positions and maintain those positions for an extended period.

Echolalia and Echopraxia

Echolalia involves the repetition of words or phrases spoken by others, while echopraxia refers to the mimicry of the movements and gestures of others. These behaviors highlight the complex disruptions in communication and motor coordination that are characteristic of catatonic schizophrenia.

Emotional Expression and Communication

Individuals with catatonic schizophrenia may exhibit reduced emotional expression, including a flat or blunted affect. Their ability to communicate effectively can be compromised by their motor disturbances and the cognitive impact of the disorder, making it challenging to engage in meaningful interactions.

Diagnosis and Differential Diagnosis

Diagnosing catatonic schizophrenia involves recognizing the presence of catatonic symptoms, which may coexist with other features of schizophrenia. It's important to differentiate catatonic schizophrenia from medical conditions that can result in similar motor disturbances, such as certain neurological disorders or metabolic imbalances.

Treatment Approaches and Challenges

The treatment of catatonic schizophrenia may involve a combination of antipsychotic medications, psychotherapy, and supportive interventions. Medications aim to alleviate the motor disturbances and other symptoms. However, treatment can be challenging due to the unpredictable nature of the catatonic episodes and the potential side effects of medication.

Creating a Supportive Environment

Support from family members, caregivers, and mental health professionals is crucial for individuals with catatonic schizophrenia. Providing a structured and safe environment, as well as offering consistent encouragement, can help individuals manage their symptoms and improve their quality of life.

Fostering Understanding and Compassion

Understanding the unique challenges posed by catatonic schizophrenia fosters empathy and compassion for those living with this subtype. By acknowledging the complexities of motor disturbances and their impact on communication and daily functioning, we contribute to a more inclusive society that supports the diverse experiences of individuals with catatonic schizophrenia. In exploring the intricacies of catatonic schizophrenia, we gain insights into the profound disruptions in movement, communication, and emotion that individuals with this subtype experience. By shedding light on this distinctive manifestation of schizophrenia, we take steps toward increasing awareness, empathy, and effective interventions that empower individuals with catatonic schizophrenia to lead meaningful lives.

Beyond Labels: The Impact of Symptom Complexity

The intertwining of positive, negative, and cognitive symptoms creates a complex and nuanced experience for individuals living with schizophrenia. These symptoms can vary in intensity and manifestation over time, contributing to the challenges individuals face in their personal and social lives. Understanding this complexity is essential for effective diagnosis, treatment, and support.

As we explore the intricate landscape of schizophrenia symptoms, we are reminded of the resilience of those who navigate these challenges daily. In the following chapters, we will further delve into the origins and causes of schizophrenia, shedding light on the factors that contribute to the emergence of these diverse symptoms. Through understanding, empathy, and knowledge, we hope to pave the way for better support, treatment, and improved quality of life for individuals living with schizophrenia.

Undifferentiated Schizophrenia: Unraveling the Complexity of Mixed Symptoms

Within the spectrum of schizophrenia, undifferentiated schizophrenia presents as a subtype characterized by a diverse range of symptoms that do not neatly fit into the criteria of other subtypes. This complexity makes undifferentiated schizophrenia a challenging condition to diagnose and manage. Understanding the nuances of undifferentiated schizophrenia is essential for comprehending its impact on individuals and guiding effective treatment approaches.

The Essence of Undifferentiated Schizophrenia

Undifferentiated schizophrenia is marked by a mix of symptoms that do not clearly align with the distinctive patterns of other schizophrenia subtypes, such as paranoid, disorganized, or catatonic schizophrenia. Individuals with undifferentiated schizophrenia may experience a combination of positive, negative, and cognitive symptoms, making their clinical presentation more varied and challenging to categorize.

Heterogeneous Symptom Profile

The hallmark of undifferentiated schizophrenia is its heterogeneous symptom profile. This can include a blend of delusions, hallucinations, disorganized thinking, emotional disturbances, and cognitive deficits. Individuals with undifferentiated schizophrenia may not fit neatly into the diagnostic criteria of other subtypes due to the diverse nature of their symptoms.

Diagnosis and Differential Diagnosis

Diagnosing undifferentiated schizophrenia involves assessing the presence of a wide range of symptoms over a significant period. It's crucial to differentiate undifferentiated schizophrenia from other conditions that can share similar symptoms, such as mood disorders, other schizophrenia subtypes, or substance-related disorders.

Treatment Challenges

Treating undifferentiated schizophrenia can be challenging due to the complex and varied nature of the symptoms. Tailoring a treatment plan to address the individual's unique combination of positive, negative, and cognitive symptoms require a comprehensive and holistic approach.

Comprehensive Treatment Approach

Treatment for undifferentiated schizophrenia often involves a combination of antipsychotic medications, psychotherapy, and psychosocial interventions. Medications aim to manage symptoms such as delusions, hallucinations, and disorganized thinking. Psychotherapy can address cognitive deficits and emotional disturbances, while psychosocial interventions focus on improving daily functioning and enhancing social interactions.

Supportive Environment

Creating a supportive environment is crucial for individuals with undifferentiated schizophrenia. Family members, caregivers, and mental health professionals play a vital role in providing consistent support, encouraging treatment adherence, and fostering understanding of complex symptomatology.

Fostering Empathy and Understanding

Recognizing the complexity of undifferentiated schizophrenia fosters empathy and understanding for those living with this subtype. By acknowledging the challenges posed by the mixed symptom profile, we contribute to reducing stigma and promoting a more inclusive society that embraces the diversity of schizophrenia experiences.

In delving into the intricacies of undifferentiated schizophrenia, we gain insights into the diverse array of symptoms that individuals with this subtype navigate. By shining a light on this complex manifestation of schizophrenia, we pave the way for greater awareness, empathy, and targeted interventions that empower individuals with undifferentiated schizophrenia to lead lives of purpose and connection.

The Medical Costs of Schizophrenia: A Complex Financial Burden

Schizophrenia is a chronic mental health disorder that not only affects individuals on a psychological and emotional level but also places a significant financial strain on both patients and society at large.

The medical costs associated with schizophrenia encompass a range of factors, including direct treatment expenses, indirect costs due to lost productivity, and the socioeconomic impact on families and communities.

Direct Treatment Costs:

Medication Expenses: Antipsychotic medications, a cornerstone of schizophrenia treatment, can be costly. While generic options may offer some relief, newer and more effective medications might come at a higher price.

Psychiatrist and Therapist Visits: Regular visits to psychiatrists, therapists, and mental health professionals are essential for effective treatment. These appointments contribute to outpatient costs.

Hospitalization: In severe cases or during episodes of acute psychosis, hospitalization may be necessary. The expenses associated with hospital stays, including medical care and room charges, can accumulate quickly.

Indirect Costs:

Lost Productivity: Schizophrenia often leads to impaired cognitive functioning and reduced ability to work or maintain employment. This results in lost income, missed career opportunities, and diminished economic productivity.

Caregiver Burden: Family members and caregivers often shoulder a significant burden, including time away from work and increased stress. This can impact their own productivity and well-being.

Unemployment Benefits and Disability: For those unable to work due to the severity of their symptoms, reliance on unemployment benefits or disability support programs becomes necessary, contributing to indirect costs.

Health and Well-Being Impact:

Physical Health Complications: Individuals with schizophrenia may experience physical health issues, such as obesity, diabetes, cardiovascular problems, and respiratory disorders. These conditions entail additional medical expenses.

Substance Abuse Treatment: Co-occurring substance abuse disorders are common among individuals with schizophrenia. Seeking treatment for substance abuse adds to the overall medical costs.

Socio Economic Impact:

Education and Vocational Services: Efforts to enhance educational attainment and vocational skills, which are critical for improving long-term outcomes, require financial investment.

Social Services: Access to social services, housing assistance, and community support programs can help individuals manage their condition and maintain stability, but these services come with associated costs.

The Financial Toll on Families:

Family Financial Strain: Families often face financial challenges due to the combination of direct and indirect costs. Caring for a loved one with schizophrenia can result in reduced income, increased medical expenses, and higher stress levels.

Reduced Savings and Retirement Plans: The financial burden of schizophrenia may lead to diminished savings, retirement plans, and long-term financial security for both individuals and their families.

Addressing the Financial Burden:

Access to Affordable Treatment: Ensuring affordable access to medications, therapies, and mental health services is crucial in alleviating the financial burden on individuals and families.

Employment and Vocational Support: Offering vocational training, job placement services, and workplace accommodations can enhance the employment prospects of individuals with schizophrenia, thereby reducing the indirect costs associated with lost productivity.

Social Safety Nets: Robust social safety nets, including disability benefits, housing assistance, and mental health support services, can provide crucial financial relief to individuals and families affected by schizophrenia.

Conclusion:

The medical costs of suffering from schizophrenia extend far beyond medication expenses, encompassing lost productivity, caregiver burden, and socioeconomic challenges.

As we strive to improve the lives of individuals living with schizophrenia, it's essential to address both the clinical and financial dimensions of the disorder.

By investing in affordable and accessible treatment, employment opportunities, and comprehensive support systems, we can mitigate the economic impact and enhance the overall well-being of those affected by schizophrenia.

Chapter 3: Beyond Genetics: Unraveling the Complex Causes of Schizophrenia

In the intricate mosaic of schizophrenia's emergence, multiple factors converge to shape the enigmatic condition. This chapter delves into the complex web of genetic predisposition, environmental influences, and neurochemical imbalances that contribute to the development of schizophrenia, highlighting the intricate interplay that gives rise to its enigmatic nature.

The Role of Genetic Predisposition: Unveiling Inherited Vulnerabilities

While no single gene is responsible for schizophrenia, a genetic predisposition plays a pivotal role. Research reveals that individuals with a family history of schizophrenia are at a higher risk of developing the disorder. Genetic variations associated with brain development, neurotransmitter function, and immune response have been identified, offering clues to the complex genetic landscape of schizophrenia.

Prenatal Factors: The Crucial Early Stages

The prenatal environment can significantly influence the risk of developing schizophrenia. Maternal infections, malnutrition, and stress during pregnancy have been linked to an increased likelihood of schizophrenia later in life. These factors highlight the critical importance of supporting maternal well-being during pregnancy to mitigate potential risks.

Early Life Experiences: Seeds of Vulnerability

Childhood adversity, trauma, and social stressors have been implicated in increasing the risk of schizophrenia. Such experiences can interact with genetic predisposition, altering brain development

and

contributing to the emergence of symptoms later in life. Understanding the impact of early life factors is crucial for both prevention and intervention strategies.

Neurochemical Imbalances: Unraveling Brain Communication

The intricate dance of neurotransmitters in the brain plays a vital role in schizophrenia. Dysregulation of dopamine, glutamate, and serotonin pathways has been linked to the disorder's symptoms. Dopamine dysregulation theory posits that an overactive dopamine system contributes to positive symptoms, while glutamate imbalances affect cognitive and negative symptoms.

Brain Structural Changes: Shaping the Schizophrenic Mind

Neuroimaging studies have revealed structural abnormalities in the brains of individuals with schizophrenia. Enlarged ventricles and reduced gray matter volume in certain brain regions are common findings. These changes provide insights into the neural circuits affected by schizophrenia and contribute to our understanding of its origins.

The Complexity of Interaction: A Multifactorial Puzzle

Schizophrenia's emergence is not solely attributed to genetics, environmental factors, or neurochemical imbalances in isolation. Instead, it's the intricate interplay of these factors that creates a perfect storm for the disorder's development. The vulnerability-stress model suggests that genetic predisposition interacts with environmental stressors, ultimately shaping the expression of symptoms.

As we unravel the intricate web of schizophrenia's causes, we gain a deeper appreciation for the complexity of its emergence. The fusion of genetic susceptibilities, early life experiences, and brain chemistry imbalances paints a multifaceted portrait of the disorder's origins.

In the chapters ahead, we will explore the diagnostic journey, the importance of early intervention, and the array of treatment strategies that offer hope for managing the complexities of schizophrenia.

Through knowledge and understanding, we strive to illuminate the path toward improved support, treatment, and a better quality of life for those touched by this enigmatic condition.

The Risk of Developing Schizophrenia: The risk factors for developing schizophrenia involves a multifaceted analysis of genetic, environmental, and neurobiological factors. While the exact cause of schizophrenia remains elusive, research suggests that a combination of these factors contributes to the development of the disorder. Here's a more detailed exploration of the risk factors:

Genetic Factors:

Family History: Individuals with a first-degree relative (parent, sibling, or child) who has schizophrenia are at a higher risk of developing the disorder themselves. The risk increases with the degree of genetic relatedness and the number of affected family members.

Genetic Predisposition: There is evidence to suggest that certain genetic variations, or combinations of genes, may increase susceptibility to schizophrenia. However, no a single gene has been identified as a direct cause of the disorder.

Environmental Factors:

Prenatal and Perinatal Factors: Adverse events during pregnancy or birth, such as maternal infections, malnutrition, or complications during delivery, have been associated with an increased risk of schizophrenia.

Stressful Life Events: Experiencing significant stress, trauma, or adversity during childhood, adolescence, or adulthood may contribute to the development of schizophrenia, particularly in individuals with a genetic predisposition.

Urban Environment: Growing up in urban areas with higher population density and less access to green spaces has been linked to an increased risk of developing schizophrenia.

This may be attributed to increased stress and limited social support.

Neurobiological Factors:

Brain Structure and Function: Abnormalities in brain structure and function have been observed in individuals with schizophrenia. These include changes in brain volume, connectivity, and neurotransmitter imbalances, particularly involving dopamine. Neurodevelopmental Factors: Disruptions in brain development during prenatal or early childhood stages may contribute to the emergence of schizophrenia later in life. Factors like synaptic pruning, myelination, and neurotransmitter development play a role.

Other Risk Factors:

Gender: Schizophrenia tends to manifest slightly earlier in males compared to females.

Additionally, males often experience more severe symptoms.

Age: The onset of schizophrenia usually occurs in late adolescence or early adulthood. However, a subtype known as late-onset schizophrenia can develop later in life.

Substance Abuse: Substance abuse, particularly during adolescence or early adulthood, can increase the risk of developing schizophrenia in individuals who are genetically predisposed.

Social Isolation: Growing up in socially isolated or disadvantaged environments can contribute to the risk of schizophrenia. Social support networks play a protective role.

Childhood Adversity: Exposure to childhood adversities, such as abuse, neglect, or bullying, can increase the risk of developing schizophrenia.

It's important to note that having one or more risk factors does not necessarily mean an individual will develop schizophrenia.

Similarly, the absence of risk factors does not guarantee immunity. Schizophrenia's development is likely influenced by a combination of genetic susceptibility and environmental triggers.

Early intervention, support, and proper treatment can significantly improve outcomes for individuals at risk of developing schizophrenia.

Identifying risk factors and addressing them proactively through interventions, healthy coping mechanisms, and early detection efforts can contribute to minimizing the impact of the disorder.

Chapter 4: Diagnosis and Early Intervention: The Crucial Steps in Understanding Schizophrenia

Amid the intricate mosaic of symptoms and causes, the journey to understanding and managing schizophrenia begins with a comprehensive diagnosis and timely intervention. This chapter delves into the diagnostic process, the challenges in identifying schizophrenia, and the pivotal role of early intervention in paving the way for effective treatment and improved quality of life.

The Diagnostic Puzzle: Unraveling the Complexity

Diagnosing schizophrenia is akin to assembling a complex puzzle with diverse pieces. Clinicians assess a range of symptoms, considering their duration, intensity, and impact on daily life. The Diagnostic and Statistical Manual of Mental Disorders (DSM-5) provides criteria for schizophrenia diagnosis, emphasizing the presence of specific symptoms and their duration.

Challenges in Diagnosis: The Mask of Other Conditions

The complexity of schizophrenia often leads to challenges in diagnosis. Its symptoms can overlap with other mental health disorders, such as bipolar disorder and major depressive disorder. Distinguishing between these conditions is crucial, as misdiagnosis can lead to inappropriate treatment and delayed interventions.

The Role of Early Intervention: Navigating the Path to Recovery

Early intervention is a cornerstone in managing schizophrenia effectively. Timely diagnosis and treatment can significantly improve long-term outcomes, reduce symptom severity, and enhance the individual's quality of life. Intervening at the onset of symptoms can prevent the progression of the disorder and mitigate potential complications.

Barriers to Early Intervention: Stigma and Access to Care

Despite the importance of early intervention, several barriers exist. Stigma surrounding mental health issues can delay help-seeking behavior. Limited access to mental health services, especially in underserved communities, can hinder individuals from receiving the care they need. Addressing these barriers is essential for ensuring that individuals with schizophrenia receive timely support.

Holistic Assessment: Beyond Symptoms Alone

Diagnosing schizophrenia goes beyond the identification of symptoms; it involves understanding the individual's unique experiences, personal history, and the impact of symptoms on daily life. Clinicians often gather information from various sources, including the individual, family members, and close friends, to form a comprehensive picture.

The Power of Diagnosis: Paving the Way for Treatment and Support

A formal diagnosis of schizophrenia is not an endpoint but rather a starting point for the journey ahead. It opens doors to tailored treatment strategies, support networks, and opportunities for psychoeducation. A clear diagnosis empowers individuals and families with knowledge, enabling them to navigate the challenges of schizophrenia more effectively.

As we navigate the intricacies of diagnosing schizophrenia, we come to realize the importance of early identification and intervention. By understanding the complexities of the diagnostic process and the challenges it poses, we are better equipped to support those who embark on the journey of managing schizophrenia. In the chapters that follow, we will explore the treatment landscape, from medications and therapies to holistic approaches, shedding light on the strategies that offer hope for managing the symptoms of this complex disorder.

Chapter 5: Treatment Strategies: Medications, Therapies, and Holistic Approaches

In the tapestry of managing schizophrenia, a range of treatment options forms the foundation for restoring balance and well-being. This chapter delves into the diverse array of strategies available, from antipsychotic medications to psychotherapies and holistic approaches, highlighting the multifaceted nature of addressing the complex symptoms of schizophrenia.

Antipsychotic Medications: Balancing Brain Chemistry

Antipsychotic medications, also known as neuroleptics, play a pivotal role in managing the symptoms of schizophrenia. These medications work by targeting neurotransmitter imbalances, particularly the excessive dopamine activity implicated in positive symptoms. First-generation (typical) and second-generation (atypical) antipsychotics offer varying mechanisms and potential side effects, requiring careful consideration in treatment selection.

Psychotherapeutic Approaches: Navigating the Inner Landscape

Psychotherapy provides individuals with schizophrenia a safe space to explore their thoughts, emotions, and coping strategies. Cognitive-Behavioral Therapy (CBT) can help manage distressing symptoms, challenge delusional beliefs, and enhance problem-solving skills. Social skills training and family therapy facilitate improved communication and interaction with others.

Psychosocial Interventions: Holistic Care for the Whole Person

Beyond medication and therapy, psychosocial interventions encompass a range of strategies to enhance an individual's overall well-being. These approaches focus on daily life skills, vocational training, and community integration. Supported employment, housing assistance, and peer support programs contribute to an individual's journey toward recovery.

Holistic Approaches: Nurturing Body and Mind

Recognizing the interconnectedness of mental and physical well-being, holistic approaches address all aspects of an individual's health. Nutrition, exercise, mindfulness, and relaxation techniques contribute to reducing stress, improving mood, and promoting overall wellness. A holistic approach recognizes that optimal health extends beyond symptom management.

The Importance of Tailored Treatment: Individualized Care Plans

Each individual's experience with schizophrenia is unique, necessitating a personalized treatment approach. Collaborative treatment planning involves engaging the individual, their family, and a multidisciplinary team of healthcare professionals. A holistic assessment considers the severity of symptoms, the impact on daily life, and personal preferences in crafting a comprehensive care plan.

The Journey of Treatment: Navigating Challenges and Celebrating Progress

The journey of managing schizophrenia is not without its challenges, but it is also marked by moments of progress, resilience, and hope. Treatment may involve adjustments to medication, exploration of various therapies, and the pursuit of self-care practices. Celebrating small victories and seeking support along the way are essential aspects of the treatment journey.

As we explore the diverse landscape of treatment strategies, we come to appreciate the multi-faceted nature of addressing schizophrenia's complexities. By delving into antipsychotic medications, psychotherapeutic approaches, and holistic interventions, we pave the way for individuals with schizophrenia to embark on a journey of healing and growth.

In the chapters ahead, we will delve into the lived experiences of individuals with schizophrenia, the role of support networks, and the efforts to challenge stigma and build understanding.

Through knowledge and compassionate care, we strive to illuminate the path toward improved well-being and a brighter future for those navigating the complexities of schizophrenia.

Medications in the Treatment of Schizophrenia: Navigating Neurochemistry

Schizophrenia, a complex mental health disorder, often requires a multifaceted treatment approach. Medications, particularly antipsychotics, play a pivotal role in managing the symptoms and improving the quality of life for individuals living with schizophrenia. These medications target the underlying neurochemical imbalances that contribute to the disorder's manifestation. Understanding the different classes of antipsychotic medications, their mechanisms of action, and potential side effects is essential for optimizing treatment outcomes.

Antipsychotic Medications: An Overview

Antipsychotic medications, also known as neuroleptics, are the cornerstone of pharmacological treatment for schizophrenia. They are divided into two main classes: typical (first-generation) antipsychotics and atypical (second-generation) antipsychotics. These medications work by affecting the balance of neurotransmitters, particularly dopamine, in the brain.

Typical Antipsychotics:

Mechanism of Action: Typical antipsychotics primarily block dopamine receptors in the brain, specifically the D2 receptors. By reducing dopamine activity, they help alleviate positive symptoms like hallucinations and delusions.

Examples: Chlorpromazine, haloperidol, fluphenazine.

Side Effects: Typical antipsychotics are associated with a range of side effects, including extrapyramidal symptoms (EPS) like tremors, rigidity, and dystonia. Tardive dyskinesia, a movement disorder

characterized by involuntary movements, can
also occur with long-term use.

Atypical Antipsychotics:

Mechanism of Action: Atypical antipsychotics
not only target dopamine receptors but also
impact other neurotransmitters such as
serotonin. They have a more balanced effect
on multiple neurotransmitter systems, which
can improve negative and cognitive
symptoms.

Examples: Risperidone, olanzapine,
quetiapine, aripiprazole, clozapine.

Side Effects: Atypical antipsychotics are
generally associated with a lower risk of EPS
compared to typical antipsychotics. However,
they can still cause weight gain, metabolic
disturbances, and, in rare cases,
agranulocytosis (a reduction in white blood
cells) with clozapine.

Treatment Considerations:

Individualized Approach: Choosing the most appropriate antipsychotic medication depends on factors such as the individual's symptom profile, medical history, potential side effects, and response to previous treatments.

Side Effect Management: Addressing side effects is crucial for long-term treatment adherence. Regular monitoring and collaboration between the individual and healthcare provider can help manage potential adverse effects.

Clozapine: Clozapine, an atypical antipsychotic, is often reserved for individuals who do not respond to other treatments. While effective, it requires close monitoring due to the risk of agranulocytosis and metabolic side effects.

Adjunctive Medications:

In addition to antipsychotics, other medications may be used to address specific symptoms or side effects of schizophrenia:

- **Antidepressants**: Used to manage co-occurring depression or anxiety symptoms.
- **Anxiolytics**: Prescribed for anxiety symptoms that may accompany schizophrenia.
- **Mood Stabilizers**: Sometimes used to manage mood fluctuations or agitation.
- **Cognitive Enhancers**: Medications like acetylcholinesterase inhibitors may be used to address cognitive deficits.

The Role of Medications in Comprehensive Treatment:

Medications are a cornerstone of schizophrenia treatment, but they are often most effective when combined with psychosocial interventions, therapy, and support networks. Collaborative treatment plans that address the physical, psychological, and social dimensions of schizophrenia contribute to improved overall outcomes and better quality of life for individuals living with the disorder.

Navigating the world of antipsychotic medications involves a partnership between individuals, caregivers, and healthcare providers. Through informed decision-making, regular communication, and adherence to treatment plans, individuals with schizophrenia can work toward managing symptoms, achieving stability, and embracing a life of possibility and connection.

The Holistic Approach to Treating Schizophrenia: Nurturing Mind, Body, and Spirit

Schizophrenia, a complex mental health disorder, requires a comprehensive treatment approach that goes beyond medications alone. The holistic approach to treating schizophrenia recognizes the interconnectedness of the mind, body, and spirit, aiming to address not only the symptoms but also the individual's overall well-being. By encompassing various dimensions of health, this approach empowers individuals with schizophrenia to achieve a more balanced and fulfilling life.

Understanding the Holistic Approach:

The holistic approach to treating schizophrenia emphasizes the importance of treating the whole person rather than solely focusing on the symptoms of the disorder. It recognizes that mental health is influenced by physical, emotional, social, and environmental factors, and seeks to create a treatment plan that takes all these factors into consideration.

Components of the Holistic Approach:

Medication Management: While the holistic approach includes various aspects of treatment, medications remain an essential part of managing schizophrenia. Antipsychotic medications help alleviate symptoms, allowing individuals to engage more effectively in other aspects of their treatment.

Psychotherapy and Counseling: Individual and group psychotherapy can provide a safe space for individuals to explore their thoughts, feelings, and coping strategies.

Cognitive-Behavioral Therapy (CBT), supportive therapy, and family therapy can help individuals manage symptoms, develop skills, and enhance their support networks.

Nutrition and Physical Health: A balanced diet and regular exercise contribute to overall well-being. Nutrient-rich foods can positively impact brain health, and exercise can help reduce stress, improve mood, and enhance cognitive function.

Sleep Hygiene: Quality sleep is essential for mental health. Establishing a consistent sleep routine and creating a conducive sleep environment can help individuals manage symptoms and improve their overall sense of well-being.

Stress Management: Techniques such as mindfulness, meditation, deep breathing, and progressive muscle relaxation can help individuals manage stress and anxiety, which can exacerbate schizophrenia symptoms.

Social Support: Building and maintaining a strong support network is crucial. Positive relationships, whether with family, friends, or support groups, provide emotional support, reduce isolation, and foster a sense of belonging.

Vocational and Educational Support: Engaging in meaningful work or education can enhance self-esteem and promote a sense of purpose. Vocational training and educational programs tailored to individual strengths and abilities can be beneficial.

Creative Expression and Leisure Activities: Engaging in creative outlets such as art, music, writing, or other hobbies can provide an avenue for self-expression, reduce stress, and boost self-esteem.

Mind-Body Practices: Practices such as yoga, tai chi, and qigong combine physical movement with mindfulness, promoting relaxation, flexibility, and mental clarity.

The Power of Personalization:

The holistic approach is inherently personalized, recognizing that every individual's journey with schizophrenia is unique. Treatment plans are tailored to the individual's specific needs, preferences, and circumstances, fostering a sense of agency and empowerment.

Family Involvement:

Incorporating family members into the holistic treatment approach is often beneficial. Family education, communication skills training, and family therapy can help improve family dynamics, enhance understanding, and create a supportive environment.

Benefits of the Holistic Approach:

The holistic approach to treating schizophrenia recognizes that individuals are more than their diagnosis. By addressing various aspects of health and well-being, this approach can lead to:

- Improved symptom management and relapse prevention
- Enhanced quality of life
- Increased self-awareness and self-empowerment
- Greater resilience and coping skills
- Strengthened social connections and support networks

A Journey of Empowerment:

The holistic approach to treating schizophrenia acknowledges that recovery is a journey, not a destination. By nurturing the mind, body, and spirit through a variety of strategies, individuals can navigate the challenges of schizophrenia with a greater sense of empowerment, resilience, and hope for the future.

Therapeutic Diet and Exercise for Individuals with Schizophrenia: Enhancing Wellness

The integration of a balanced diet and regular exercise into the treatment plan for individuals with schizophrenia can offer a range of physical, mental, and emotional benefits.

The synergy between diet and exercise contributes to overall well-being, potentially improving symptoms, reducing medication side effects, and enhancing the individual's quality of life.

Diet for Schizophrenia: Nourishing the Mind and Body

A well-rounded diet rich in nutrients can have a positive impact on both physical and mental health for individuals with schizophrenia:

Omega-3 Fatty Acids: Omega-3 fatty acids found in fatty fish, flaxseeds, and walnuts have been associated with improved cognitive function and mood regulation. Incorporating these foods may contribute to better mental well-being.

Antioxidant-Rich Foods: Foods high in antioxidants, such as colorful fruits and vegetables, can help combat oxidative stress and inflammation, potentially benefiting brain health.

Complex Carbohydrates: Whole grains and complex carbohydrates provide a steady release of glucose, which is essential for brain function. They also promote stable energy levels and mood.

Lean Proteins: Lean protein sources, such as poultry, fish, legumes, and low-fat dairy, provide essential amino acids that support neurotransmitter production and overall mental health.

B Vitamins: B vitamins, particularly B6, B9 (folate), and B12, play a role in brain health. Consuming foods rich in these vitamins, such as leafy greens, beans, fortified cereals, and lean meats, can be beneficial.

Limit Sugar and Processed Foods: Reducing the intake of sugary foods and highly processed items can help stabilize blood sugar levels and prevent energy crashes.

Exercise for Schizophrenia: Energizing the Mind and Body

Regular physical activity can have profound effects on mental health and symptom management for individuals with schizophrenia:

Mood Enhancement: Exercise releases endorphins, which are natural mood boosters. Engaging in physical activity can reduce feelings of anxiety, depression, and stress.

Cognitive Benefits: Regular exercise has been shown to improve cognitive function, including attention, memory, and executive skills. This can be particularly valuable for addressing cognitive deficits often associated with schizophrenia.

Social Engagement: Participating in group exercises or classes can provide opportunities for social interaction, reducing feelings of isolation and promoting a sense of belonging.

Stress Reduction: Physical activity can help individuals cope with stress by promoting relaxation and enhancing the body's stress response mechanisms.

Sleep Quality: Regular exercise can improve sleep quality, which is crucial for mental health. Adequate sleep supports mood stability and cognitive function.

Personalized Approach:

Consultation with Healthcare Professionals: Before making significant changes to diet and exercise, individuals with schizophrenia should consult their healthcare provider. This ensures that modifications align with their specific needs and health conditions.

Gradual Implementation: Small, gradual changes to diet and exercise routines are often more sustainable and achievable.

Setting realistic goals and tracking progress can be motivating.

Holistic Wellness:

Integration with Other Treatments: A therapeutic diet and exercise plan should complement other components of the treatment plan, including medication and therapy.

Mindfulness and Self-Care: Practices such as mindfulness meditation, yoga, and relaxation techniques can enhance the holistic benefits of diet and exercise, supporting mental and emotional well-being.

Family and Social Support:

Involvement of Support Network: Encouraging participation in physical activities and adopting a balanced diet can be a collaborative effort involving family members, friends, and caregivers.

Conclusion:

Incorporating a therapeutic diet and regular exercise into the lifestyle of individuals with schizophrenia can contribute to improved physical health, cognitive function, mood regulation, and overall well-being.

This holistic approach, when personalized and integrated into the treatment plan, empowers individuals to take an active role in managing their condition and enhancing their quality of life.

Chapter 6: Living with Schizophrenia: Personal Journeys of Resilience and Hope

Within the intricate mosaic of schizophrenia's challenges lies the strength, resilience, and hope of individuals who navigate its complexities with courage. This chapter shares personal stories and experiences of those living with schizophrenia, illuminating their triumphs, struggles, and strategies for coping in the face of adversity.

Voices of Resilience: Navigating the Uncharted Territory

The journey of living with schizophrenia is often marked by unexpected twists and turns. Personal narratives shed light on the initial onset of symptoms, the search for answers, and the process of coming to terms with a diagnosis. These stories capture the resilience of individuals who navigate the uncharted territory of a condition that can be isolating and bewildering.

Challenging Stigma: Breaking Silence and Building Understanding

Living with schizophrenia often entails facing the stigma that surrounds mental health issues. Individuals share their experiences of discrimination, misconceptions, and the power of advocacy. By sharing their stories, they challenge stereotypes and contribute to changing perceptions about schizophrenia and those who live with it.

Navigating Relationships: Family, Friends, and Support Networks

Personal journeys highlight the role of relationships in the lives of individuals with schizophrenia. Families and friends provide invaluable support, but their efforts can also be accompanied by challenges. Individuals recount the ways in which understanding, empathy, and open communication fostered stronger relationships, allowing them to lean on those closest to them.

Coping Strategies: Tools for Navigating Daily Life

Living with schizophrenia requires adapting to the ebb and flow of symptoms. Personal stories reveal a wide range of coping strategies, from mindfulness and art therapy to journaling and music. These tools empower individuals to manage stress, alleviate anxiety, and find solace amidst the complexities of their experiences.

Pursuing Goals: Triumphs, Ambitions, and Celebrating Progress

Despite the challenges of living with schizophrenia, individuals continue to pursue their goals and aspirations. Whether pursuing education, pursuing a career, or engaging in creative pursuits, their stories reflect the power of determination and the impact of a supportive environment.

The Power of Peer Support: Finding Connection and Belonging

Peer support plays a pivotal role in the lives of individuals with schizophrenia. Support groups, online communities, and advocacy organizations provide spaces for shared experiences, understanding, and encouragement. Personal narratives underscore the importance of finding connection and belonging among those who have walked a similar path.

A Message of Hope: Embracing the Journey

Through their stories, individuals living with schizophrenia offer a message of hope to others facing similar challenges. Their journeys illustrate that while living with schizophrenia may present obstacles, it does not define one's worth or potential. By sharing their experiences, they inspire others to embrace their journey, seek support, and pursue a fulfilling life.

As we listen to the voices of those living with schizophrenia, we gain a profound understanding of the depth of their experiences.

These personal narratives provide insights into the challenges faced and the strategies employed to navigate a life touched by schizophrenia.

In the chapters ahead, we will further explore the role of support networks, address stigma, and examine stories of triumph and resilience that offer inspiration and guidance for those who embark on a similar journey.

Chapter 7: Building a Supportive Network: The Role of Family, Friends, and Community

Amid the complexities of living with schizophrenia, a strong support network plays a pivotal role in shaping the journey towards well-being. This chapter delves into the importance of family, friends, and community in providing understanding, compassion, and the necessary tools to navigate the challenges of schizophrenia.

The Family Dynamic: Understanding and Empathy

Families often serve as the primary source of support for individuals living with schizophrenia. This section explores the emotions and experiences family members may undergo as they grapple with their loved one's diagnosis. Understanding and empathy become essential tools in fostering open communication and reducing the impact of stigma within the family unit.

Caregiver Challenges: Navigating the Complex Terrain

Caregivers of individuals with schizophrenia face unique challenges. Balancing their own well-being with providing support and care can be overwhelming. From managing medications to facilitating therapy sessions, caregivers require a comprehensive understanding of the disorder's nuances, strategies for self-care, and resources for seeking assistance.

The Role of Friends: Allies in the Journey

Friendships can serve as a crucial buffer against isolation for individuals with schizophrenia. Friends who offer understanding, patience, and companionship play a pivotal role in creating a sense of belonging and acceptance. Personal stories highlight the significance of true friendships that transcend the barriers created by the disorder.

Community Support: Bridging Isolation

Community organizations, support groups, and advocacy networks provide a sense of belonging beyond personal relationships. These spaces offer opportunities for individuals with schizophrenia to connect with peers who share similar experiences, fostering a sense of understanding and solidarity. Community initiatives also challenge stigma and promote awareness.

Promoting Open Dialogue: Enhancing Communication

Effective communication between individuals with schizophrenia and their support networks is vital. Strategies for fostering open dialogue, active listening, and nonjudgmental conversations are explored. Creating an environment where individuals feel comfortable expressing their experiences can contribute to improved well-being and a deeper sense of connection.

Navigating the Journey Together: Allies in Recovery

Recovery from schizophrenia is a collective journey that involves not only the individual but also their support network. Celebrating progress, acknowledging challenges, and fostering an atmosphere of collaboration contribute to a sense of shared accomplishment. By uniting efforts, families, friends, and communities become allies in the pursuit of well-being.

Fostering Resilience: The Transformative Power of Support

The stories shared in this chapter illuminate the transformative power of a supportive network. Family members, friends, and community allies contribute to fostering resilience, empowerment, and a sense of hope. By amplifying understanding and offering unwavering support, these networks shape a brighter future for individuals living with schizophrenia.

As we explore the vital role of family, friends, and community in the lives of individuals with schizophrenia, we come to understand that a strong support network is an anchor in the midst of challenges. The bonds forged within these networks foster understanding, challenge stigma, and offer a lifeline of empathy and empowerment. In the chapters ahead, we will continue to shed light on efforts to combat stigma, celebrate stories of recovery, and explore the advancements in schizophrenia research that contribute to a more hopeful future.

Support Groups

. BC Schizophrenia Society

. NAMI Connect recovery Support

. Schizophrenia.com

. Hearing Voices Network

. National Paranoia Network

. Schizophrenia Alliance

. Rethink Mental Illness

. themighty.com

Chapter 8: Shattering Stereotypes: Challenging the Stigma Surrounding Schizophrenia

In the shadows of stigma, the journey of individuals with schizophrenia often unfolds with added challenges. This chapter delves into the pervasive stigma that surrounds mental health issues, examines its impact on those living with schizophrenia, and explores efforts to break down misconceptions and foster understanding.

The Weight of Stigma: Navigating Misconceptions

Stigma surrounding schizophrenia is a powerful force that can isolate individuals, perpetuate misunderstandings, and impede their access to care. Misconceptions about the disorder often contribute to fear, discrimination, and a lack of empathy.

Challenging these misconceptions becomes essential for creating an environment of understanding.

Media Influence: From Portrayals to Perception

Media plays a significant role in shaping societal perceptions of schizophrenia. From sensationalized depictions in movies to news stories that focus on negative incidents, media can perpetuate stereotypes and contribute to the fear and misunderstanding associated with the disorder. Recognizing and critiquing these portrayals is a step towards dismantling stigma.

The Ripple Effect: Impact on Daily Life

Stigma doesn't exist in isolation; its effects reverberate through various aspects of an individual's life. Employment opportunities may be limited, relationships strained, and self-esteem diminished.

The fear of judgment can deter individuals from seeking help, leading to delayed treatment and prolonged suffering.

Empowerment Through Education: Dispelling Myths

Educational efforts become a potent tool in challenging stigma. By dispelling myths about schizophrenia, providing accurate information, and fostering a climate of open discussion, individuals and communities can gain a better understanding of the disorder. Initiatives that focus on education reduce fear and encourage empathy.

The Role of Personal Narratives: Sharing Stories, Changing Minds

Personal stories offer a unique opportunity to humanize the experience of living with schizophrenia. Individuals who openly share their journeys become advocates for change, dismantling stereotypes through their narratives. These stories help bridge the gap between those with lived experiences and those seeking to understand.

Breaking the Silence: Advocacy and Awareness

Challenging stigma requires collective efforts. Advocacy organizations, mental health professionals, and individuals with schizophrenia unite to challenge stereotypes, promote awareness, and foster empathy. Campaigns that humanize the disorder and highlight the potential of those living with it contribute to a culture of acceptance.

Shaping a Stigma-Free Future: The Way Forward

Efforts to combat stigma offer a glimpse of a more inclusive and understanding future. By addressing media portrayals, promoting education, and fostering open dialogue, we take steps towards erasing the stigma associated with schizophrenia. Embracing a culture of empathy and acceptance paves the way for improved support and well-being.

As we confront the issue of stigma surrounding schizophrenia, we are reminded of its far-reaching impact and the urgent need for change.

Through education, open conversations, and shared narratives, we lay the foundation for a future in which individuals with schizophrenia can live without the burden of judgment and fear.

In the chapters ahead, we will delve into the stories of recovery, explore advancements in research, and reflect on the potential for a more inclusive society that embraces the humanity of all its members.

A Personal Story

Patrick: "I was a straight-A student. I studied a lot, had a great group of friends and even had a girlfriend I loved. Life was good.

Then, everything changed. It was as if a light switch had been flipped overnight.

I broke up with my girlfriend, which was a dark moment for me. Yet instead of emerging from that sadness like most high schoolers do, I felt like a different person. I was paranoid, thinking that my classmate could hear my innermost thoughts. And I was told that my sentences had become 'word salad'.

I also became superstitious about everything. You know how kids will say things like, "If you step on a crack, you will break your mother's back? I had thoughts like that a lot, and I'd see hallucinatory messages in numbers and letters, believing that they had some type of hidden meaning.

Not surprisingly, all of this made me really anxious. I couldn't think clearly and retreated to my bedroom, refusing to come out. At first, my parents and friends didn't know what to think. I'm sure they hoped I was going through a weird phase. But when weeks passed and something was clearly still going on with me, my mom took me to see a psychiatrist. Those were some of the scariest moments of my life. Imagine that one day you can think clearly and the next, you are delusional, although I didn't even realize it at the time. Eventually, I was diagnosed with paranoid schizophrenia. In one way, that news was terrifying. Hearing you have a mental illness that you'll have to deal with forever is really hard to wrap your head around. But if I'm honest, my diagnosis also filled me with relief. At least I had some answers to why everything I had ever known suddenly became distorted. At least there was hope that I might have some sense of normalcy again.

My psychiatrist talked to me about an LAI medicine that provides a month's worth of treatment with just one dose. Not having to take medication every day meant I wouldn't accidentally skip or double up on a dose, and it just felt simpler not having to take medications every day. So after my doctor talked to me about the upsides and possible side effects, I started taking the injectable.

I did really well with the injectable medication.

When you have schizophrenia, finding a medication that works for you is a game-changer. For me, it felt like my life's greatest blessing. It's hard to put to words how relieved you feel when you can finally think straight.

In the Spring of 2015, I graduated with a degree in mathematics from California State University. Soon after, I was hired as a system analysis intern.

Chapter 9: Advancements and Hope: Research, Treatment Innovations, and Future Possibilities

Within the realm of schizophrenia, research and innovation pave the way for brighter horizons. This chapter explores the ongoing advancements in understanding the disorder, the evolving landscape of treatment strategies, and the potential future possibilities that offer hope to individuals living with schizophrenia.

The Landscape of Research: Unveiling the Unknown

Advancements in neuroscience, genetics, and imaging technologies have shed light on the intricate workings of the brain in schizophrenia. Researchers explore the underlying biological mechanisms, seeking to unravel the genetic factors, neurochemical imbalances, and brain structural changes that contribute to the disorder's complexity.

Personalized Treatment Approaches: Tailoring Care

The concept of personalized medicine is gaining ground in schizophrenia treatment. Genetic profiling and biomarker research hold the potential to guide treatment decisions, ensuring that interventions are tailored to an individual's unique profile. This approach aims to optimize treatment effectiveness and minimize side effects.

Emerging Therapies: Beyond Traditional Approaches

Innovations in psychotherapy and psychosocial interventions continue to expand the treatment landscape. Cognitive remediation therapy targets cognitive deficits, helping individuals improve their cognitive function and daily life skills. Virtual reality therapy offers immersive experiences for managing symptoms and enhancing emotional regulation.

Holistic Strategies: Integrating Mind and Body

Holistic approaches gain recognition for their potential to improve well-being in schizophrenia. Nutritional interventions, exercise programs, mindfulness practices, and yoga contribute to reducing stress, promoting relaxation, and enhancing overall health. The integration of mind-body practices recognizes the interconnected nature of well-being.

Hope on the Horizon: Investigating New Avenues

Cutting-edge research explores novel avenues in schizophrenia treatment. NMDA receptor modulators, targeting glutamate imbalances, show promise in managing cognitive symptoms. Gene therapy and deep brain stimulation hold potential for altering brain function and mitigating symptoms. These potential breakthroughs offer hope for improved outcomes.

Bridging Research and Practice: The Path to Implementation

Translating research findings into practical interventions is a crucial step. Collaborations between researchers, clinicians, individuals with lived experiences, and advocacy organizations are essential in bringing advancements from the laboratory to the clinical setting. Bridging this gap ensures that individuals benefit from the latest research.

Advances in Research in the Treatment of Schizophrenia: Pioneering New Horizons

The field of schizophrenia research has made significant strides in understanding the underlying mechanisms of the disorder and developing innovative treatment approaches. As our knowledge deepens, researchers are uncovering new insights into the neurobiology of schizophrenia, refining existing treatments, and exploring novel interventions that hold promise for improving the lives of individuals living with the disorder.

Neurobiological Insights:

Neuroinflammation: Research has highlighted the role of neuroinflammation in schizophrenia. Chronic inflammation in the brain can contribute to cognitive deficits and symptoms. Investigating immune system dysregulation has led to new avenues for treatment development.

Neuroplasticity: Neuroplasticity, the brain's ability to adapt and reorganize, is being explored as a potential target for interventions. Modulating neural circuits through techniques like transcranial magnetic stimulation (TMS) holds promise for symptom improvement.

Glutamate Modulation: Glutamate, a major neurotransmitter, is being investigated for its role in schizophrenia. Medications targeting glutamate receptors, such as NMDA receptor modulators, are being studied as potential add-on treatments to antipsychotics.

Personalized Medicine:

Genetic Profiling: Advances in genetics have allowed researchers to identify specific genetic variations associated with schizophrenia. Genetic profiling may help tailor treatment approaches to an individual's unique genetic makeup.

Pharmacogenomics: Pharmacogenomic research aims to match medications with an individual's genetic profile, optimizing treatment efficacy while minimizing side effects. This approach holds promise for more personalized and effective treatment plans.

Cognitive Enhancement:

Cognitive Remediation: Cognitive deficits are a core aspect of schizophrenia. Cognitive remediation programs aim to improve attention, memory, and executive functions through computer-based training and behavioral interventions.

Targeting Negative Symptoms: Addressing negative symptoms such as social withdrawal and reduced emotional expression remains a challenge. New interventions, including cognitive-behavioral therapies focused on social cognition, aim to improve functional outcomes.

Digital Therapeutics:

Mobile Apps and Wearables: Digital tools, such as smartphone apps and wearable devices are being developed to support individuals with schizophrenia. These tools can assist with medication adherence, mood tracking, cognitive training, and symptom management.

Virtual Reality Therapy: Virtual reality (VR) therapy is being explored as a way to create controlled environments for exposure therapy, helping individuals confront and manage their fears or delusional beliefs.

Neuroimaging Advances:

Functional MRI (fMRI): Functional MRI techniques allow researchers to observe brain activity patterns in individuals with schizophrenia. This has led to insights into the neural mechanisms underlying symptomatology and response to treatment.

Connectomics: Connectomics, the study of neural networks and connectivity in the brain, has provided insights into disruptions in communication between brain regions in schizophrenia. This knowledge may guide targeted interventions.

Early Intervention:

Prodromal Detection: Researchers are investigating early signs and risk factors for schizophrenia, with the goal of identifying individuals at risk and providing interventions to prevent or mitigate the onset of full-blown symptoms.

Early Psychosis Clinics: Specialized clinics offer early intervention services, combining medication, psychotherapy, and psychosocial support to address symptoms during the critical early stages of the disorder.

Integrative Approaches:

Mind-Body Interventions: Yoga, mindfulness meditation, and other mind-body practices are being studied for their potential to complement pharmacological treatments and improve overall well-being.

Nutritional Interventions: Research into the role of nutrition and gut health in schizophrenia is emerging. Understanding the gut-brain connection may lead to novel approaches for symptom management.

Challenges and Future Directions:

While advances in research hold promise, challenges remain. Developing interventions that target specific symptoms, minimizing side effects, and ensuring access to innovative treatments are ongoing priorities. Additionally, understanding the complex interplay of genetic, environmental, and neurobiological factors requires further investigation.

Conclusion:

The landscape of schizophrenia treatment is evolving rapidly due to groundbreaking research. As researchers continue to unravel the complexities of the disorder's biology, cognitive impairments, and social challenges, new treatments that address the diverse aspects of schizophrenia are emerging.

By embracing a multidisciplinary and innovative approach, the field is paving the way for more effective, personalized, and holistic interventions that empower individuals to live meaningful and fulfilling lives despite the challenges posed by schizophrenia.

Embracing Possibilities: A Future of Potential

Advancements in research and treatment strategies inspire a sense of hope and possibility for individuals living with schizophrenia. As science continues to unravel the mysteries of the disorder, the potential for earlier diagnosis, more effective interventions, and improved quality of life becomes increasingly attainable.

As we explore the advancements and possibilities within the realm of schizophrenia, we are reminded of the power of knowledge, innovation, and collaboration.

The ongoing efforts of researchers, healthcare professionals, individuals with lived experiences, and advocacy organizations contribute to a future where individuals living with schizophrenia can access effective, personalized, and holistic treatments.

In the chapters that follow, we will reflect on the collective journey, the transformation of perspectives, and the potential for a society that embraces the diversity of human experiences.

Chapter 10: A Vision of Inclusion: Building Understanding and Fostering Change

In the culmination of our exploration of schizophrenia, a vision emerges—a vision of an inclusive society that embraces empathy, understanding, and the diverse human experience. This chapter reflects on the collective journey we've undertaken, the transformations we've witnessed, and the steps we can take to create a world that supports and uplifts individuals living with schizophrenia.

Embracing Diversity: Redefining Normalcy

The journey of understanding schizophrenia has illuminated the spectrum of human experiences. By embracing diversity in mental health, we redefine what it means to be "normal." The stories of resilience, the insights from research, and the

advocacy efforts

remind us that every individual's journey is valid and valuable.

Challenging Stigma: Advocacy in Action

The fight against stigma has garnered momentum, inspiring individuals, communities, and institutions to challenge stereotypes and misconceptions. Advocacy efforts have led to policy changes, increased access to care, and shifts in societal attitudes. By continuing to amplify voices and break down barriers, we move closer to a stigma-free world.

Creating Inclusive Communities: The Role of Education

Education becomes a cornerstone in fostering an inclusive society. Schools, workplaces, and communities benefit from mental health education that promotes understanding, empathy, and effective communication. Empowering individuals with accurate information equips them to provide meaningful support and challenge stigma.

A Lifeline of Support: Building Stronger Networks

Family members, friends, and support networks form a vital lifeline for individuals with schizophrenia. By nurturing open conversations, understanding the needs of those living with the disorder, and offering unconditional support, we create environments where individuals can thrive and pursue their aspirations.

Promoting Holistic Well-Being: Mind, Body, and Spirit

The integration of mental, physical, and emotional well-being becomes a central tenet in creating a supportive society. Holistic approaches, including self-care practices, mindfulness, and wellness programs, contribute to individuals' overall health, fostering resilience and empowerment.

Cultivating Compassion: A Call to Action

Creating an inclusive society requires a collective commitment to cultivating compassion. By practicing active listening, offering a helping hand, and standing up against discrimination, we demonstrate our dedication to building a world where individuals with schizophrenia are valued, heard, and supported.

A Vision of the Future: Hope and Possibility

As we conclude this journey through the intricate landscape of schizophrenia, we envision a future where the stigma is dismantled, where research leads to breakthroughs, and where each individual's potential is celebrated. This future is built on a foundation of empathy, understanding, and the unwavering belief that together, we can shape a world that fosters well-being for all.

The vision of inclusion we've explored in this chapter is a call to action for each of us. By fostering understanding, challenging stigma, and embracing the uniqueness of every individual, we contribute to a society where the human experience, in all its dimensions, is valued and respected. In the pages that follow, we reflect on the profound impact of our collective efforts and the potential for a world where those touched by schizophrenia are empowered to lead lives of purpose, connection, and hope.

Family Support for Individuals with Schizophrenia: Nurturing Resilience Together

Schizophrenia affects not only the individual diagnosed but also their family members. The support and understanding provided by family play a crucial role in the overall well-being, treatment adherence, and recovery of the person living with schizophrenia. By adopting a compassionate and informed approach, family members can create an environment that fosters resilience, empowerment, and meaningful connections.

Education and Understanding:

Learn about Schizophrenia: Educate yourself about the nature of schizophrenia, its symptoms, treatment options, and potential challenges. Understanding the disorder helps dispel misconceptions and promotes empathy.

Communication: Open and honest communication is key. Create an environment where the individual feels comfortable discussing their experiences, feelings, and treatment goals without fear of judgment.

Emotional Support:

Empathy and Validation: Acknowledge the individual's experiences and emotions. Validating their feelings can provide comfort and reduce feelings of isolation.

Active Listening: Listen actively and without interruption when the individual chooses to share. This fosters trust and helps them feel understood and supported.

Treatment Collaboration:

Involve in Treatment Decisions: Encourage the individual to actively participate in treatment decisions. Be supportive without imposing your preferences, as their needs and preferences may evolve over time.

Medication Management: Assist in medication adherence by helping the individual establish a routine, organizing medications, and providing reminders.

Monitor for side effects and communicate with healthcare professionals.

Creating a Supportive Environment:

Structure and Routine: Establish a consistent daily routine that includes sleep, meals, and activities. Predictability can help reduce anxiety and provide a sense of stability.

Safe Space: Create a safe and calm environment at home. Minimize stressors and conflicts that may trigger or exacerbate symptoms.

Encouraging Independence:

Setting Realistic Goals: Help the individual set achievable goals, whether related to education, work, or personal interests. Celebrate their successes and encourage resilience in the face of setbacks.

Skills Development: Support the individual in developing life skills, such as managing finances, maintaining personal hygiene, and practicing social interactions.

Reducing Stigma:

Promote Understanding: Educate extended family members, friends, and the community about schizophrenia. This helps reduce stigma and creates a more inclusive social network.

Advocacy: Advocate for the individual's rights and needs within the community, healthcare system, and educational institutions.

Self-Care for Caregivers:

Emotional Resilience: Caregivers need support too. Seek counseling, support groups, or therapy to manage your own emotional well-being and prevent burnout.

Balance: Find a balance between supporting your loved one and maintaining your own needs, interests, and relationships.

Crisis Management:

Crisis Plan: Develop a crisis plan with the individual, outlining steps to take in case of a relapse or severe symptom exacerbation. This plan can include contacts for mental health professionals and emergency services.

Early Warning Signs: Familiarize yourself with the individual's early warning signs of relapse. This allows for timely intervention and support.

Seeking Professional Help:

Professional Guidance: Collaborate with mental health professionals to understand the best ways to support the individual's treatment plan, manage symptoms, and address challenges.

Family Therapy: Participate in family therapy sessions if recommended. This can improve communication, resolve conflicts, and enhance the family's ability to support the individual.

Patience and Unconditional Love:

Unwavering Support: Your presence, patience, and unconditional love are among the most valuable forms of support you can offer. Remember that recovery is a journey, and your steadfast presence matters.

Celebrate Progress: Celebrate even small achievements and milestones on the individual's recovery journey. Acknowledging progress fosters motivation and optimism.

By adopting these approaches, family members can create a foundation of unwavering support for individuals living with schizophrenia. This support plays a pivotal role in enhancing treatment outcomes, reducing the impact of symptoms, and fostering a sense of belonging and empowerment.

Conclusion: Navigating the Complexities of Schizophrenia

In the pages of this book, we embarked on a journey through the intricate landscape of schizophrenia—a journey marked by challenges, insights, and profound moments of understanding. We delved into the depths of the disorder, exploring its origins, symptoms, diagnostic journey, treatment strategies, and the transformative power of human stories. From the scientific breakthroughs to the personal narratives, we uncovered the multifaceted nature of schizophrenia and the resilience of those who live with it.

We began by peering into the enigmatic world of schizophrenia, where genetic predispositions intertwine with environmental factors to shape its emergence. The chapters unfolded, revealing the complexities of diagnosis, the significance of a supportive network, and the power of challenging

stigma. We celebrated the advancements in research,

the promise of innovative treatments, and the potential for a future where understanding prevails over ignorance.

The stories shared within these pages remind us that behind the diagnosis lies a journey of triumph, resilience, and hope. We've walked alongside individuals who navigated the labyrinth of symptoms, who shattered stereotypes, and who defied the limitations imposed by the disorder. We've seen the strength that emerges from the support of family, friends, and community, and we've witnessed the transformation that comes from challenging stigma and advocating for change.

Our exploration has led us to envision a world that embraces the diversity of human experiences, where compassion replaces judgment and empathy drives understanding. As we close this chapter, we are reminded that the journey doesn't end here—it continues with each interaction, conversation, and effort to create a more inclusive society. By embracing the complexities of schizophrenia and fostering a culture of acceptance, we move closer to a future where individuals living with the disorder can thrive, pursue their dreams, and contribute to a world enriched by their unique perspectives.

In the echoes of the stories shared and the knowledge gained, we find the power to shape a brighter future. Let us take the lessons learned from these pages and translate them into actions that uplift, empower, and transform.

Together, we have the capacity to make a difference, to navigate the complexities of schizophrenia with grace, and to build a world that stands united in compassion and understanding.

References

Schizophrenia: Diagnosis and treatment. (07Jan2020); MayoClinic. Retrieved from www.mayoclinic.org

What Is Schizophrenia: Symptoms, causes, diagnosis and treatment. (14 July 2022); EverydayHealth. Retrieved from www.everydayhealth.com

www.ingramcontent.com/pod-product-compliance
Lightning Source LLC
Chambersburg PA
CBHW050819260726
48660CB00004B/1516